THE PRACTICAL STRATEGIES SERIES
IN GIFTED EDUCATION

series editors
FRANCES A. KARNES, PH.D., & KRISTEN R. STEPHENS, PH.D.

Identifying and Nurturing Math Talent

M. Katherine Gavin, Ph.D.

Routledge
Taylor & Francis Group

NEW YORK AND LONDON

First published 2011 by Prufrock Press Inc.

Published 2021 by Routledge
605 Third Avenue, New York, NY 10017
2 Park Square, Milton Park, Abingdon, Oxon OX14 4RN

Routledge is an imprint of the Taylor & Francis Group, an informa business

ISBN 13: 978-1-59363-833-7 (pbk)

Contents

The Practical Strategies Series in Gifted Education offers teachers, counselors, administrators, parents, and other interested parties up-to-date instructional techniques and information on a variety of issues pertinent to the field of gifted education. Each guide addresses a focused topic and is written by an individual with authority on the issue. Several guides have been published. Among the titles are:

- *Acceleration Strategies for Teaching Gifted Learners*
- *Curriculum Compacting: An Easy Start to Differentiating for High-Potential Students*
- *Enrichment Opportunities for Gifted Learners*
- *Independent Study for Gifted Learners*
- *Motivating Gifted Learners*
- *Questioning Strategies for Teaching the Gifted*
- *Social & Emotional Teaching Strategies*
- *Using Media & Technology With Gifted Students*

For a current listing of available guides within the series, please contact Prufrock Press at 800-998-2208 or visit http://www.prufrock.com.

In its 2010 report, *Preparing the Next Generation of STEM Innovators: Identifying and Developing Our Nation's Human Capital*, the National Science Board reported one fundamental concept: "The U.S. education system too frequently fails to identify and develop our most talented and motivated students who will become the next generation of innovators" (p. 5).

Two decades ago, a challenge was issued by the nation's governors and heralded by then President George H. Bush: By the year 2000, United States students would be first in the world in mathematics and science achievement. Yet in 2008, our international test scores in mathematics showed that while more than 40% of fourth and eighth graders in Singapore and other Asian countries scored at the most advanced level in mathematics, only 10% of U.S. fourth graders and 6% of U.S. eighth graders scored at this level (National Center for Education Statistics, 2008). Results from the National Assessment of Educational Progress (NAEP, 2009) indicated that only 6% of fourth graders and 8% of eighth graders performed at the advanced level. It is at this level that eighth graders are expected to use abstract thinking, the foundation for high-level mathematics.

It is clear that we are not doing a good job of helping our talented math students achieve at high levels. Yet in order to be globally competitive, that is exactly what we need to do. Today more than ever, we need to produce top-notch mathematicians in order to maintain our leadership as a world power. The numbers in this category are dismal, and there are few rising stars on the horizon. Recent statistics show that fewer than 1% of students who graduate from college have completed their major in mathematics (National Center for Education Statistics, 2010). To remedy this, we must start identifying mathematical talent early. Then we need to work hard to provide talented students with a challenging curriculum that will fuel their passion for math and their desire to continue studying mathematics throughout college, as well as inspire them to choose a math-related career field.

Jake is a bright ninth grader. He loves thinking about and working with shapes. He can transform a three-dimensional shape using reflections and rotations in his mind and predict the images faster than his classmates, even when they are using physical models. For fun, he enjoys designing spaces and thinks he might like to become an engineer or an architect.

Michelle, a third grader, loves everything about numbers. She really shines at algebraic reasoning. Her teacher is amazed at how fast she can come up with a general pattern for a number sequence. These patterns are often so sophisticated that her teacher needs to take time to think about them to fully understand them.

Twelve-year-old Latoya has a unique way of approaching some problems. She often comes up with an idea that no one has thought of, including her teacher! She also thinks of unusual questions that not only touch on the math at hand, but go way beyond. She loves working on independent math projects that explore topics like fractals and nanotechnology that are not in her math book.

If you ask 20 different educators to define mathematical talent, you will get a variety of different answers (maybe even 20). In fact, there may be administrators and teachers who have never stopped to consider what this talent actually encompasses. This is evident in the way students are identified as having math talent. Some school districts focus on test scores, such as IQ scores, or on standardized achievement test results, including national tests such as the Iowa Tests of Basic Skills, the EXPLORE, the SAT, the ACT, and local district tests. Other school districts use classroom performance and report card grades in mathematics. Elementary teachers often look for quick recall of basic facts and facility with computation as evidence of mathematical talent. Yet researchers have found that speed in doing mathematics is secondary to mathematical insight (Davidson & Sternberg, 1984). A different approach to identifying mathematical talent is to focus on problem solving and mathematical reasoning ability, looking for an inquisitive and intuitive mathematical mind that considers the world from a mathematical perspective (Krutetskii, 1968/1976). The reality is that in order to identify mathematical talent, there first needs to be a working definition of what that talent is.

Different Types of Mathematical Minds

One reason mathematical talent is so difficult to define is that there are different types of mathematical minds. Vadim Krutetskii, a Russian psychologist, was interested in finding out just what mathematical talent was. Doing work similar to that of Jean Piaget, he observed many students in the process of doing mathematics. He found that he could categorize students with mathematical talent into three types: those with an "algebraic cast of mind," thinking and acting very abstractly; those with a "geometric" mind, whose talent lies in their spatial visualization and reasoning ability; and those who demonstrate a combination of these two types. This division of talent may be relatively easy for most people to relate to as they think about their high school math courses. Some people enjoyed more, and performed better in, algebra courses than their high school geometry courses. Krutetskii concluded from his observations that, although useful, neither speed, nor facility in computation, nor the ability to memorize formulas are necessary requirements for math talent.

The Task Force on Mathematically Promising Students

Particularly in the United States, the definition of mathematical talent is more complicated, as students have varying levels of opportunities to be exposed to mathematics at home and at school. A student may have strong reasoning ability, yet not have been given the opportunity to think about interesting, high-level problems. This is especially evident with students of poverty. The National Council of Teachers of Mathematics (NCTM), the driving force in Pre-K–12 mathematics curriculum and instruction in the United States, established a task force in 1994 to examine issues regarding mathematical talent and to make recommendations concerning identification and programming. The task force chose to use the term "mathematically promising" rather than gifted or talented to emphasize the goal of including students who previously may have been excluded due to their lack of opportunity or exposure to challenging mathematics. This definition is an outgrowth of the broadened definition of giftedness that the federal government issued with the passage of the Javits Gifted and Talented Students Education Act in 1988. The task force proceeded to define mathematically promising students as "those who have potential to become leaders and problem solvers of the future" (Sheffield, Bennett, Berriozabal, DeArmond, & Wertheimer, 1999, p. 310). They defined mathematical promise as

> a function of ability, motivation, belief, and experience or opportunity. This definition includes the students who have been traditionally identified as gifted, talented, precocious, and so on, and it adds students who have been traditionally excluded from rich mathematical opportunities. This definition acknowledges that students, who are mathematically promising, have a large range of abilities and a continuum of needs that should be met. (Sheffield et al., 1999, p. 310)

Identifying Mathematical Talent and Talent Potential

The ultimate goal of identification of mathematical talent should be to provide services to students to nurture their talent. With that in mind, if we use the four criteria that the NCTM task force recommends to identify students with talent and talent potential, we cannot focus solely on mathematics achievement. If we do so, we may miss students who have creative problem-solving abilities seldom evidenced on multiple-choice tests. If we don't think about motivation, we will certainly miss students who, with the right teacher and the kind of mathematics that is relevant to their daily lives and their interests, can display mathematical talent that is far beyond what their test scores indicate. If we don't notice those who have been traditionally overlooked and may lack belief in themselves, we may miss students with math talent potential. Finally, we must recognize that there are students who have not been given rich mathematical problems to consider and thus have not been able to demonstrate their math talent. This is true not only of some students of poverty, but also of many other students who have been exposed to mathematics as a set of procedures and rules to memorize, and who have never had the opportunity to solve real math problems that require high-level thinking.

Multiple Measures for Identification

Clearly, no single instrument is able to identify all students with talent or talent potential. There are three important factors to consider when creating an identification process:

- there are different types of math talent,
- multiple measures should be used to provide a variety of sources of information, and
- students should be given the opportunity to demonstrate talent at different times over multiple time periods (Gavin, 2005).

The focus should be on an identification *process*, rather than a *procedure*. The process needs to be ongoing, with flexible entry points for students to receive different types of services, and the instruments used can include both test data and more informal descriptive information.

Tests can include:

- standardized achievement tests such as the Iowa Tests of Basic Skills and state mastery tests;
- reasoning ability tests designed specifically for talented students, such as the *Test of Mathematical Abilities for Gifted Students* (TOMAGS);
- out-of-level ability tests such as those used in national talent searches, the Scholastic Aptitude Test (SAT), The Secondary School Admission Test (SSAT-L), and the EXPLORE test developed by the American College Testing Program (ACT); and
- nonverbal ability tests such as the Cognitive Abilities Test (CogAT). These types of tests are particularly useful with English language learners, as they are mainly pictorial and require little or no reading.

Descriptive information can include:
- interviews with students and observations of students engaged in mathematical problem solving,
- analysis of performance tasks completed by students involving challenging problems,
- classroom performance and report card grades, and
- rating scales to identify behavioral characteristics that manifest math talent.

To access more detailed research supporting these measures, see Gavin and Adelson (2008).

Descriptive measures are inherently biased, as the person observing, interviewing, or rating the student decides how and what to report. Nevertheless, such measures can add a valuable dimension to the identification process. It is important to consider the behavioral characteristics of students doing math. What do they do when confronted with a real math problem, one for which they do not have an immediate solution? What kinds of questions do they ask? What strategies do they employ? To address these issues, some mathematics educators have developed a checklist of observable behaviors. These are frequently developed based on experiences with students, and they sometimes use the literature on gifted math students.

The best resources on the characteristics of mathematically gifted students are research-based. There are many available, including the Gifted Evaluation Scale (GES-2; McCarney & Anderson, 1998), the Gifted and Talented Evaluation Scales (GATES; Gilliam, Carpenter, & Christensen, 1996), the Purdue Academic Rating Scales (PARS; Feldhusen, Hoover, & Sayler, 1989) for secondary students, and the more recent Math Scales for Rating the Behavioral Characteristics of Superior Students (Gavin, 2010). This last scale, shown in Figure 1, is an addition to the Scales for Rating the Behavioral Characteristics of Superior Students (Renzulli, Smith, White, Callahan, & Hartman, 1976), which have undergone several revisions and are still one of the most widely used scales in gifted education. The math scale was

Scales for Rating the Behavioral Characteristics of Superior Students

Student's Name (or Assigned Code No.) _____

(please fill in)

MATHEMATICS CHARACTERISTICS
© 2003 M. Katherine Gavin

The student . . .

	Never	Very Rarely	Rarely	Occasionally	Frequently	Always
1. is eager to solve challenging math problems (A problem is defined as a task for which the solution is not known in advance).	☐	☐	☐	☐	☐	☐
2. organizes data and information to discover mathematical patterns.	☐	☐	☐	☐	☐	☐
3. enjoys challenging math puzzles, games, and logic problems.	☐	☐	☐	☐	☐	☐
4. understands new math concepts and processes more easily than other students.	☐	☐	☐	☐	☐	☐
5. has creative (unusual and divergent) ways of solving math problems.	☐	☐	☐	☐	☐	☐
6. displays a strong number sense (e.g., makes sense of large and small numbers, estimates easily and appropriately).	☐	☐	☐	☐	☐	☐
7. frequently solves math problems abstractly, without the need for manipulatives or concrete materials	☐	☐	☐	☐	☐	☐
8. has an interest in analyzing the mathematical structure of a problem.	☐	☐	☐	☐	☐	☐
9. when solving a math problem, can switch strategies easily, if appropriate or necessary.	☐	☐	☐	☐	☐	☐
10. regularly uses a variety of representations to explain math concepts (written explanations, pictorial, graphic, equations, etc.).	☐	☐	☐	☐	☐	☐

	Never	Very Rarely	Rarely	Occasionally	Frequently	Always
Add Column Total:	☐	☐	☐	☐	☐	☐
Multiply by Weight:	1	2	3	4	5	6
Add Weighted Column Totals:	☐ +	☐ +	☐ +	☐ +	☐ +	☐
Scale Total:						☐

Figure 1. Mathematics scales for rating the behavioral characteristics of superior students.

From *Scales for Rating the Behavioral Characteristics of Superior Students* (3rd ed., p. 48), by J. S. Renzulli et al, 2004, Mansfield Center, CT: Creative Learning Press. Copyright © 2010 by Creative Learning Press. Reprinted with permission.

piloted by teachers who rated more than 726 students in grades 4–6 in urban, suburban, and rural settings with a reliability of .98 (Renzulli, Siegle, Reis, Gavin, & Sytsma Reed, 2009). It has been used successfully along with other measures to identify elementary students for talented math programs in national research studies funded by the U.S. Department of Education and afterschool math enrichment programs.

Using this broadened definition of math talent and multiple ways to identify talent, teachers should consider themselves to be math talent scouts on the lookout for new students with talent and talent potential, rather than gatekeepers to the gifted math program (Gavin, 2005). With teachers having this attitude, we hope to see many more students accessing rich mathematics that can nurture their talent and provide the challenge and motivation they deserve.

Once Identified, What's Next?

If we examine how teachers and schools are developing mathematical talent, we may find that there are as many different ways to nurture talent as there are ways to define it. The first and foremost consideration in providing services to talented students is matching the type of instruction with the individual needs of the student. In addition to different types of mathematical talent, there is a range of mathematical talent, from students who learn mathematics quickly and easily to extremely precocious students who can generalize and make abstractions at a very early age. Services (i.e., curriculum, instruction, programming) need to be differentiated depending on where a student fits in this spectrum of talent. Some advocate acceleration for the brightest of students and enrichment for those students who need a little more than the regular curriculum. However, this solution is too simplistic, and it is not an appropriate way to look at providing services. Acceleration is defined as moving through the curriculum at a more rapid pace. Enrichment is defined as providing more in-depth or extended experiences of the math content. There are advantages and challenges with both types of programming, but the bottom line is that a combination of both approaches is the richest and most appropriate way to nurture talent.

Talented students need more than the regular grade-level curriculum, and they also need a curriculum that is characterized by rigor, challenge, and in-depth reasoning, which is often not provided by simply accelerating the student into the next grade level's textbook program.

Acceleration

Because of the linear progression in the learning of math skills and procedures, acceleration should be considered when providing appropriate services for mathematically talented students. Acceleration also has a great deal of research support. The Templeton National Report on Acceleration, *A Nation Deceived: How Schools Hold Back America's Brightest Students* (Colangelo, Assouline, & Gross, 2004), provides a very thorough review of different types of acceleration and the research supporting the various options. For students who are extremely precocious in mathematics, acceleration—most likely radical acceleration including skipping grade levels and math courses—should be the baseline for providing services. With regard to acceleration, consider the following practices, which have proven research effectiveness:

- *Early entrance to school in kindergarten or first grade.* This is one of the smoothest solutions with regard to developing math talent, as gaps in skills and math knowledge are minimized.
- *Grade skipping.* This is appropriate when a student is advanced in many content areas. Many parents worry about the social or emotional development of their child if he or she skips a grade and so has peers who are 1–2 years older. Research has shown that neither early entrance to school nor grade skipping harm children (Robinson & Weimer, 1991; Rogers, 1992). In fact, it is just the opposite. When students are in a curriculum

that is too low level and socialize with their age peers, they can become social outcasts (VanTassel-Baska, 2005). Instruments such as the *Iowa Acceleration Scale* (Assouline, Colangelo, Lupkowski-Shoplik, Lipscomb, & Forstadt, 2003) are available to help parents and teachers make informed decisions on whether acceleration in terms of grade skipping is an appropriate option.

- *Subject-matter acceleration.* It is interesting that many elementary teachers believe that a student who is talented in reading and language arts will also be talented in mathematics. This is not necessarily the case, just as the reverse is not necessarily true either. Therefore, subject-matter acceleration is often the more appropriate option. There are different ways to do this. In elementary school, students can move to the next grade level during math time. In higher grades, students can take 2 or more years of math in 1 year. Another option is for students to receive credit for a course by taking the final examination of course material. Many high school students have International Baccalaureate (IB) programs, Advanced Placement (AP) courses, and/or college courses available to them in which they can receive college credit. In recent years, we have seen distance learning and online courses become popular. These options allow students to stay in their home schools and still take accelerated courses.

Considerations With Acceleration

There are some considerations and challenges with accelerating students in mathematics. One is very practical. It is not always easy for students to have the opportunity to take a higher level math class. Physically moving to a different classroom or building is not always easy to arrange. Often, math is not taught at the same time at the next grade level, or there is no transportation to move a student to a different building where the higher level program is taught. Although these are obstacles, teachers, administrators, and parents should work together to find a solution. Simply put, it is unfair to keep a student in a program in which he or she already knows the material.

In addition, merely advancing a student to the next grade level's math program, or even advancing the student two grade levels, is no guarantee that the program is providing the rigor and challenge that talented students need and deserve. The regular curriculum is generally written for the "average" math student, and its pace and depth are often not sufficient to meet the needs of talented students. If they remain in one of these programs, talented students learn all of the necessary mechanics earlier and faster, but they do not have an opportunity to explore the reasons for the rules or to tackle more challenging problems. They need acceleration along with a different, advanced curriculum.

Advanced Placement (AP) courses, once thought to meet the needs of the most talented students at the high school level, are now being called into question in terms of their effectiveness in this role. In fact, Advanced Placement courses were never designed specifically for gifted students. Instead, they are college courses that are offered to high school students, originally intended for motivated seniors. The National Research Council (NRC; 2002) found four concerns regarding AP courses that are relevant for the education of talented math students: conceptual understanding is often not stressed; cooperative projects are not encouraged; application of knowledge to new situations is not emphasized; and the validity of the AP exams has been questioned, especially with regard to the lack of high-level thinking required on the exams. The NRC's report (2002) recommended that both the AP and the IB mathematics programs align better with current research on learning by enhancing conceptual development and including interdisciplinary content while decreasing the emphasis on covering content in order to allow for deeper exploration.

Does this mean we should not offer these courses to our top students? Of course not. They are advanced courses. However, AP and IB teachers need to be aware that top students need more challenge and a deeper exploration of mathematics than may be prescribed in the syllabi for these curricula. Encouraging classroom discussions that promote high-level thinking focusing on justification, reasoning, creative solutions to problems, and problem posing will escalate the level of challenge. Adding problems, projects, and writing assignments that go beyond the prescribed course requirements will also enhance these courses.

Additionally, many online and summer programs provide advanced courses. In fact, Subotnik, Edmiston, and Rayhack (2007) found that unless a school has specialized curricula, including research seminars or apprenticeship programs, almost all advanced talent development happens after school and during the summer. Keep in mind that these programs often involve considerable expenses. There are some scholarships available, and being creative and persistent can certainly pay off. A list of some national programs that provide out-of-school opportunities, including distance learning courses, is available in the resources section of this book.

There are challenges when providing talented math students with opportunities. However, there are ways to rise to these challenges. It is important for administrators, teachers, counselors, and parents to work together to ensure that the accelerated course of study that a student pursues is the right one for him or her. Especially if these courses are outside of the regular district curriculum, an agreement should be reached beforehand so that these courses will be acknowledged and the student will advance to the next appropriate course in the curriculum when entering back into the school district's math program.

Here is a final word of caution regarding seeking appropriate accelerated mathematics for talented students. A student misses out on an important part of the mathematical learning experience when he or she is not given an opportunity to communicate with others (peers, teachers, or mentors) in terms of engaging in rich mathematical discussions that foster both critical and creative thinking. There are times when one needs to think alone about how to solve a hard mathematics problem. There are other times when one needs to talk about and build upon ideas with others, listen to and learn other strategies, and work together to solve and even create new mathematics. Talented students of all ages deserve to have a chance to do both in any course of study.

Enrichment

The word *enrichment* means different things to different people, even textbook authors. These meanings can range from an enrichment worksheet, which is something akin to busy work, such as a crossword puzzle with math terms, to an extension project based on a student's area of interest, such as the mathematics of fractals, their occurrence in nature, and their use in solving world problems. There are many supplementary materials available, including books, software programs, and websites that teachers use as enrichment. There are also specific curricula written for talented mathematics students. Other enrichment opportunities that lie outside of the school environment are described later on.

Mentoring, in particular working with a mathematics professor on a research project or meeting on a regular basis to explore an advanced topic of interest, is another way to enrich talented students. There are many mathematics professors who find joy in nurturing a mathematical mind and working with someone, albeit much younger, who is as passionate about mathematics as they are.

Math internships, either during or after school, especially with professionals who use high-level mathematics in their careers (e.g., actuaries, engineers, computer programmers) and with research mathematicians also offer excellent opportunities to stimulate talented students and encourage them to pursue mathematics in college and beyond.

Considerations With Enrichment

The number one challenge when providing enrichment as an add-on to the regular curriculum is the concern that it may not be truly rigorous or challenging for students. There are too many supplementary resources that are just not mathematically rich. Having students complete enrichment worksheets by themselves that only take them a short period of time often means that the work is too easy. Moreover, resources such as logic puzzles, nonroutine problems, and math games that are certainly fun and can even be challenging still do not offer the type of in-depth, coherent, focused study of a math topic that our talented math students deserve. Although these activities constitute a type of enrichment, they should be given *in addition to* a special, rigorous curriculum meant to challenge talented students.

Curriculum for Talented Students

So what should the curriculum look like? Essentially, it should be a combination of accelerated and enriched content. In addition, it should be research-based, showing evidence of achievement gains for talented students that are greater than gains made by talented students in other programs using different curricula. There are many commercial units that are marketed for gifted math students, but very few have any research showing such results.

The optimal curricular model, whether it be for advanced kindergarten students or seniors in high school, should be a combination of accelerated content (accelerated to the degree that is appropriate for the student) that is enriched with in-depth, inquiry-based mathematical investigations. These investigations should foster critical and creative thinking within the context of solving rigorous mathematical problems. The curriculum should also encourage deep mathematical discussions triggered by high-level questions raised by the teacher, the students, and/or the written material. Students should have opportunities to write about the mathematics they are using to explain their thinking, justify their answers, and pose new problems to solve. Talented

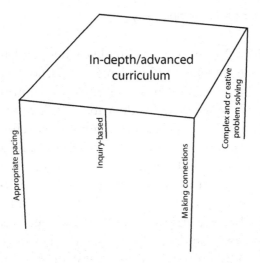

Figure 2. A model for the development of an advanced, in-depth curriculum.

From *The Peak in the Middle: Developing Mathematically Gifted Students in the Middle Grades* (p. 58), by M. Saul, S. Assouline, and L. Sheffield, 2010, Reston, VA: National Council of Teachers of Mathematics. Copyright © 2010 by the National Council of Teachers of Mathematics. All rights reserved. Reprinted with permission.

students need to engage in discussion and writing at a level that will challenge them to think hard about difficult and interesting mathematical problems. These are the kind of processes that mathematicians engage in, and we want our talented students to begin early to experience the how-to process of doing mathematics. We hope that in doing so, they will develop a passion for the subject and become our mathematicians of the future.

To summarize, Gavin and Sheffield (2010) outlined a model for advanced, in-depth curricula for middle school students that is in fact appropriate for all talented students. The model consists of four components: creative and complex problem solving, connections within and across content areas and across a variety of contexts, an inquiry-based approach akin to the practices of mathematicians, and appropriate pacing (see Figure 2).

The Importance of Starting Early

Consider Doreen, a talented middle school student. She was selected to be one of only 12 students in her school to take algebra in the seventh grade. She was essentially skipping the typical seventh- and eighth-grade mathematics. Prior to this, she had been in heterogeneous classes throughout her schooling. She was one of the smartest students in the class, always getting the right answers easily and before everyone else. She already knew most of what the teacher was teaching. Her homework took her less than 20 minutes. She was ready for algebra! But something happened when she arrived in algebra class. She was now in a class full of smart students. She was learning something new every day, and she needed to make sense of mathematics on a continual basis. She was asked questions for which she didn't know the answers right away. She didn't even know where to begin on some of them. Her teacher said this was the fun part of math—working on hard problems that you didn't know the answer to right away—but she wasn't really so sure of that. She was starting to think she was no longer smart in math.

The math curriculum can adhere to all of the previously listed criteria, but if a student hasn't been challenged early on with appropriate curriculum, it may be too late. This may be the case with Doreen, who is at an especially vulnerable adolescent age. This type of rigorous, inquiry-based curriculum, where problems are true *problems* that need time to percolate in order to be solved, needs to happen early on in a student's schooling. Students need to experience the thrill of solving hard problems and practice the strategies that mathematicians use in their daily work. They need to come to love this type of challenge and be ready and eager for more as they move ahead in their study of mathematics.

A Glimpse at Challenging Investigations Across the Grades

The activities described in this section are samples of investigations that provoke high-level mathematical thinking and pique talented students' curiosity and creativity. They are very different from a page of three-digit multiplication and division problems or an exercise on factoring complicated polynomials. All of them require students to grapple with a challenging and very interesting problem, discuss and write about their thinking, and justify their answers. This is truly how mathematicians work.

Pre-K–Grade 2

The following is a primary-level geometry investigation from the National Science Foundation's *Project M²: Mentoring Young Mathematicians* on sorting and classifying shapes. This is advanced curriculum for primary students that requires students to be able to describe the properties of shapes and to see the relationships among different shapes.

In this investigation from the unit, *Exploring Shape Games: Geometry With Imi and Zani* (Gavin, Casa, Chapin, & Sheffield, 2011), students help Imi and Zani, their bird friends from the Amazon, create shape games for children all over the world. In this particular activity, students use a set of label cards and a set of attribute shapes. There are four shapes (circles, squares, triangles, and hexagons). Each type of shape comes in three different colors (white, black, and gray) and two different sizes (big and little). The attribute label cards are shown in Figure 3.

Students take turns putting labels on intersecting loops and then filling the loops with the appropriate shapes. Figure 4 details what a Venn diagram might look like as the activity gets underway.

After playing the game, students are given a Think Deeply question to write about (see Figure 5). This question focuses on the big mathematical ideas of the unit and is intended to have students think deeply about the mathematics and grapple with classifying and sorting shapes using the sophisticated representa-

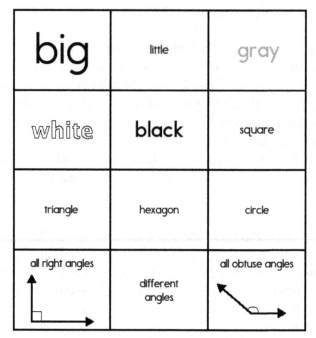

Figure 3. Attribute shape label cards.

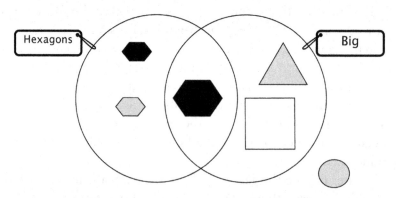

Figure 4. Model of a Venn diagram.

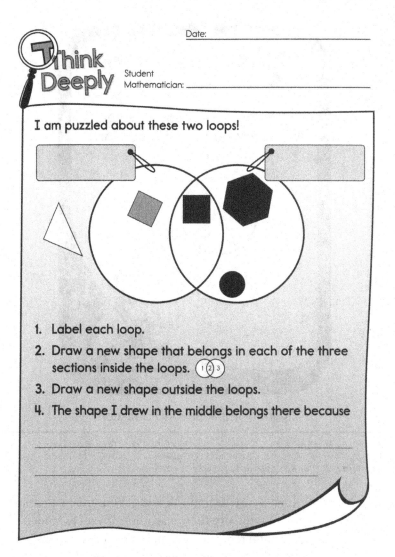

Figure 5. Think Deeply question.

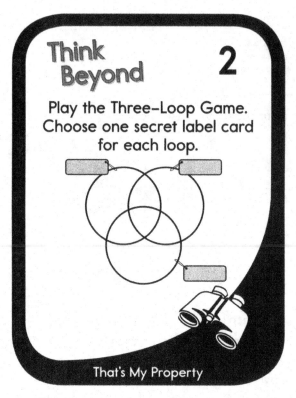

Figure 6. Think Beyond question.

From *Project M²: Exploring Shape Games: Geometry With Imi and Zani* (Teacher's Guide, p. 183), by M. K. Gavin, T. M. Casa, S. Chapin, and L. J. Sheffield, 2011, Dubuque, IA: Kendall Hunt. Copyright © 2011 by Kendall Hunt. Reprinted with permission.

tion of a three-loop Venn diagram. Writing about the mathematics and being asked to justify their reasoning advances students' understanding through reflection on their own ideas, a high-level metacognitive skill. Putting thoughts into writing is a step above and beyond verbalizing thinking. It helps students solidify their understanding and develops appropriate use of mathematical vocabulary. Justifying their thinking also encourages them to make explicit their understanding of the mathematics.

For a greater challenge, students can complete the activity on the Think Beyond card, as depicted in Figure 6.

In a national field test, Project M^2 research results showed highly significant gains from pre- to posttesting for first-grade students on this unit. In addition, Project M^2 students significantly outperformed a comparison group of students on these concepts (Carroll, 2010). See the resource section of this book for additional information on Project M^2 materials.

Grades 3–5

The following is a probability investigation for talented elementary students exploring experimental and theoretical probability from the *Project M^3: Mentoring Mathematical Minds* unit *What Are Your Chances?* (Gavin, Chapin, Sheffield, & Dailey, 2008).

In this introductory unit on probability designed specifically for mathematically talented elementary students, students learn about the likelihood of events, the Law of Large Numbers, experimental and theoretical probability, and fair and unfair games based on probability. These topics are advanced topics for elementary students. The culminating project for their study of probability is to create a Carnival of Chance to raise money for a local charity. The carnival will consist of different types of games. These games need to appear fair so that the carnival-goers will want to play, but in reality, they must be unfair so that rather than giving away prizes, the students will be collecting money for their charity—an intriguing challenge for students!

The Odd or Even game is an example of an activity from the probability unit. In this game, two players must spin each of the spinners and find the sum of the two numbers they land on. If the sum is odd, one player gets a point. The other player gets a point if the sum is even. First, students are asked to predict if the game is fair just by looking at spinners similar to the ones shown in Figure 7.

In our discussions with young students, we found that some think the game is fair because students get to take turns. Other students think it is unfair because there are four numbers on one spinner and only three on the other. Still others think it might

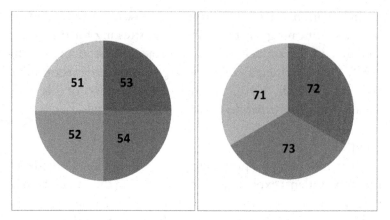

Figure 7. Odd or even spinners.

be unfair because there are four even numbers and only three odd numbers.

Next they play the game in pairs, with each student spinning 16 times. They collect class data and again discuss the fairness of the game. They use the results of their experiment to calculate experimental probabilities, and they consider the Law of Large Numbers. Finally, they realize that they need to find all possible sums and see if there is an equally likely chance of getting an even sum as there is of getting an odd sum (i.e., theoretical probability) in order to determine fairness.

Once they determine that the game is indeed fair, they are given a Think Deeply question to write about:

> *How could you change the rules of the game (keeping the spinners the same) to make it an unfair game? Using probability, explain why the change makes the game unfair.*

Project M³ was funded by the U.S. Department of Education Javits Gifted and Talented Students Education Act. Research results indicate highly significant gains from pre- to posttesting on this unit (Gavin, Casa, Adelson, Carroll, Sheffield, & Spinelli, 2007) and highly significant gains over a comparison group of

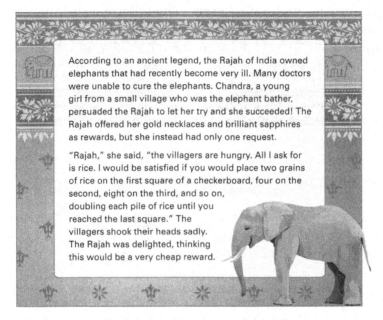

According to an ancient legend, the Rajah of India owned elephants that had recently become very ill. Many doctors were unable to cure the elephants. Chandra, a young girl from a small village who was the elephant bather, persuaded the Rajah to let her try and she succeeded! The Rajah offered her gold necklaces and brilliant sapphires as rewards, but she instead had only one request.

"Rajah," she said, "the villagers are hungry. All I ask for is rice. I would be satisfied if you would place two grains of rice on the first square of a checkerboard, four on the second, eight on the third, and so on, doubling each pile of rice until you reached the last square." The villagers shook their heads sadly. The Rajah was delighted, thinking this would be a very cheap reward.

Figure 8. Chandra's reward.

From *Solve It: Focusing on Equations, Inequalities, and Exponents* (p. 142), by M. K. Gavin, L. J. Sheffield, & S. H. Chapin, 2010, Dubuque, IA: Kendall Hunt. Copyright © 2010 by Kendall Hunt. Reprinted with permission.

students in a national field test (Gavin, Casa, Adelson, Carroll, & Sheffield, 2009).

Project M³ curriculum units—including *What Are your Chances?*—have won the National Association for Gifted Children's outstanding curriculum award from 2004–2009.

Middle Grades

An interesting and challenging algebra problem in which students discover the power of exponential functions begins with the folktale in Figure 8 from India.

This investigation is taken from a prealgebra unit called *Solve It: Focusing on Equations, Inequalities, and Exponents* (Gavin, Sheffield, & Chapin, 2010). This unit is part of *Math Innovations*, a new middle-grades math program for all students with a focus on mathematical reasoning and Think Beyond challenges for talented students. After reading the story, students are asked to think about, discuss, and write about the following questions:

What do you think? Was this a wise decision on Chandra's part? Defend your answer. In your answer, explain how this relates to exponential functions.

Think Beyond questions that extend student thinking about the function $y = 2^x$ include the following:

Predict the shape of the following graphs and how they each compare to the graph of $y = 2^x$.
   a. $y = 2 \cdot 2^x$
   b. $y = 2^{-x}$
   c. $y = \left(\frac{1}{2}\right)^x$
   d. Graph each equation on the same axes. Refine or add on to your predictions as needed.

High School
   In summarizing the way all high school education for gifted students should be organized, Dixon, Gallagher, and Olszewski-Kubilius (2009) stated that curriculum and programming need to be designed to "build motivation through engagement" (p. 182). With respect to secondary mathematics, Sriraman and Steinthorsdottir (2008) indicated that this curriculum is the gateway for an exposure to both breadth and depth of math topics, yet most secondary curricula are still taught in a traditional way devoid of a modeling-based approach used in the real world. Kerr (1997) also asserted that high school is the gatekeeper to more advanced study of mathematics. She stated that the traditional mathematics curriculum so often taught has no or very little emphasis on mathematical modeling, peer interaction, or communication. This curriculum has historically discouraged girls from taking 4 years of high school mathematics. Topics

such as transformational geometry, spherical geometry, topology, graph theory, combinatorics, and statistical modeling can spark the interest of talented students and open up interesting new avenues to explore.

The secondary curriculum *SIMMS Integrated Mathematics, Level 3* (Montana Council of Teachers of Mathematics, 2006) has an interesting chapter on spherical geometry, a type of non-Euclidean geometry that is rarely studied in high school. It begins by posing the following problem:

Imagine yourself on board an airplane flying from Los Angeles to Tokyo. What route should the pilot choose to travel the shortest distance between these two cities?

In Euclidean geometry, it is well known that the shortest distance between two points is a straight line. Here, students are challenged to think about the shortest distance between two points on a sphere, a real-world problem in the aviation industry. They then explore how other geometric terms are defined on spheres and compare this to Euclidean geometry. In the process, they gain a much deeper understanding of the Euclidean geometry they have studied since elementary school, and they are exposed to a new, fascinating type of geometry where things do not work in quite the same way. For example, in spherical geometry, a triangle can have three right angles!

In the chapter assessment, they are asked to explain how degrees of latitude and longitude are determined for a point on the Earth's surface, a real-world application of the new mathematics they have learned. They use latitude and longitude to describe a triangle on the Earth's surface for which the sum of the measures of the interior angles is 270 degrees. They are also asked to think about whether or not a line of latitude satisfies the definition of a line in spherical geometry and to defend their answer.

Teacher Qualifications

A curriculum that is mathematically challenging and motivational for students is only one piece of the puzzle. The teacher is another equally important piece. Teachers who teach mathematics to talented students must have the mathematical background necessary to pose challenging problems and high-level questions and to engage in discourse with students that helps them think deeply about the mathematics being studied. They need to be able to answer questions that go beyond the mathematics in the lesson and guide students to explore new areas of mathematics that arise from discussions. In short, they must be competent and confident with mathematics. They should also love mathematics. If you take a moment to remember a teacher you consider one of your best, no matter what subject area, you will remember that he or she truly loved the content, cared deeply about students, and wanted to instill a similar passion for the subject in students. That is why they were great teachers!

Most high school math teachers are well qualified in their subject areas, many with a major in mathematics. However, as many as one half of middle school math teachers and many elementary teachers do not have strong math backgrounds, lacking a major or minor in mathematics (Kuenzi, 2008). Most of them are more comfortable with, and have as their strength areas, reading and language arts. These include teachers of the gifted. In fact, the most qualified teachers of talented math students in grades K–12 should have a background in gifted education as well as a strong background in mathematics (National Science Board, 2010). They should also be knowledgeable about how to use math education and gifted education instructional strategies, and they should be willing to take risks and explore topics, problems, and concepts that are new to them as well as their students. If they love mathematics, these last criteria come easily. The good news is that with professional development including workshops, conferences, and coursework, teachers can learn new high-level mathematics as well as exemplary practices in both gifted education and mathematics education.

There are a variety of programming options in which curriculum and instruction for talented math students can take place. They include both school-based programs and extracurricular opportunities.

Specialized Schools

As the national focus turns more and more to science, technology, engineering, and math (STEM) education, there are many math/science magnet schools opening, both public and private, and some are designated specifically for talented students. There is research underway by the National Research Center on the Gifted and Talented and the National Science Foundation to gather information on these schools and to evaluate their effectiveness. It will be important to pay close attention to the findings of this research, for there is a range of excellence among these schools. The top specialty schools are the high schools that were created with an emphasis on math and science for talented students, such as the Illinois Math and Science Academy and the North Carolina School of Science and Mathematics. These often have teachers with doctorates in their disciplines and resident scientists and/or mathematicians who work with students on an individual basis.

Differentiation

Differentiation is a common educational buzzword these days. It is an instructional strategy designed to meet the needs of each child in a teacher's classroom. Dr. Carol Tomlinson (1995), the leading expert on differentiation, describes differentiation as "consistently using a variety of instructional approaches to modify content, process, and/or products in response to learning readiness and interest of academically diverse learners" (p. 80). Notice that this definition implies that differentiating instruction is not something to be done occasionally, but rather that it is a way of teaching that should become part of a teacher's philosophy and style of instruction. It follows from an educational belief that is simple in its statement, and yet profound in its implication.

Each student deserves and needs to learn something new in mathematics class each and every day.

It would be hard to find someone who would argue with this simple mantra. Teachers who plan and carry out their instruction using this simple mantra are pros at using differentiation. Differentiation has gotten the most attention in elementary school, where students usually spend the majority of their days in one classroom. But the practice of making sure that each student is appropriately challenged should be a goal of every K–12 teacher.

Differentiation should begin with some type of pretest to determine what students already know in the material that is going to be taught. For students who have grasped most of the concepts, it doesn't make sense to teach these concepts again. Using curriculum compacting techniques (Reis, Burns, & Renzulli, 1992), teachers can work with students to learn any skills and procedures that have not been learned as evidenced on the pretest and then move them on to new material. Many of these students need to learn this new material in a qualitatively different way than other students. They need more challenge and more rigor appropriate for more advanced mathematical minds. Thus, simply moving them along faster in the regular grade-level text is inadequate.

Flexible Grouping

It is important to reiterate that teachers need to use different instructional strategies with higher level materials with talented students. How do they do this if these students are in a classroom of 20 or more students? One way is to create cluster groups of more advanced students and then provide them with different learning experiences using different curriculum, such as the ones described previously. Flexible grouping, especially in the early grades, is a good way to ensure that students with math talent are identified and serviced throughout the year. Math talent can be nurtured and can develop at different times and in different circumstances. As mentioned earlier, teachers need to be talent scouts, always on the lookout for a student who displays creative mathematical thinking.

Flexible grouping starts with pretesting by math topic or unit to identify which students can compact out of the unit and study more advanced material. Sometimes these students are different, and so the group composition can change. For example, teachers may find that some students are more adept with number sense and number concepts and need more advanced units in these areas, while other students may be more advanced in spatial thinking and need more advanced geometry concepts. For those students who pretest out of the entire grade-level curriculum using an end-of-year test, acceleration of one or more grade levels is appropriate *along with* a curriculum that is more advanced than the regular curriculum taught at above grade level.

Ability Grouping

Differentiation also can occur between classes. This is more common in middle and high school, where honors classes offer students advanced mathematics. This generally begins in sixth or seventh grade, with a prealgebra class, and continues through high school, with Advanced Placement classes. It is important to note that these honors classes should be using different curriculum than the regular classes. The class should not just be moving faster through the same textbook. The problems should be richer, the concepts should be explored in more depth, justification and proof should be emphasized, and creative extensions should be investigated.

Ability grouping can also occur in elementary school in different ways. Students can be grouped between classes within a grade level and also across grade levels. Unfortunately, ability grouping has gone out of vogue in elementary schools for a number of reasons. Critics believe that ability grouping labels children, and they worry about the effect that ability grouping will have on students in low-ability groups. In fact, some research has shown that students in low-ability-grouped math classes do not make any greater achievement gains than students with the same ability in heterogeneous classes. However, what is often left out of the argument is the research showing that *high-ability* math students benefit greatly from being grouped together and their achievement gains are significant (Gavin, Casa, Adelson, et al., 2009; Rogers, 1992; Tieso, 2002). In fact, Gavin, Casa, Adelson, et al. (2009) found that between-class groupings of talented math students in third, fourth, and fifth grades, coupled with a specifically designed advanced mathematics curriculum for these students, resulted in highly significant gains over a comparison group of like-ability students from the same schools. So there is no reason not to group talented math students together, and there is every reason to do so, provided that the curriculum they study is advanced and appropriate for them. Dr. Karen Rogers (1991), who has studied the effects of grouping on talented students, sums it up quite effectively:

> It is very clear that the academic effects of a variety of long and short-term [homogeneous] grouping options for both the purposes of enrichment and acceleration are extremely beneficial for students who are academically or intellectually gifted or talented. There is *no* body of evidence that "the research says" otherwise! (pp. 25–26)

Pull-Out Programs and Enrichment Clusters

Other programming options in schools include pull-out programs and enrichment clusters. Pull-out programs can be used for full-time math instruction. In effect, this constitutes a gifted math class on a daily basis, where students with talent learn their mathematics similarly to how they would in an ability-grouped class. Pull-out programs can also be used for math enrichment, an add-on to the regular math class. These classes generally meet once or twice a week. If the regular math class is truly differentiated and students are learning advanced mathematics, then these additional pull-out classes can provide stimulating math experiences focusing on students' interest areas outside of the curriculum being studied.

However, many pull-out programs are the only differentiated mathematics instruction that talented students receive. In this case, they are truly not enough, but can still provide challenging and rigorous instruction if appropriate curriculum is used. We recommend that this be more of a focused, coherent study of a particular topic that goes on for 4–6 weeks in biweekly sessions. This gives students some exposure to the type of mathematics they should be studying. To keep students focused on a topic for this length of time, the material needs to be motivational and must generate rich discussion and writing opportunities (see the resources section for a list of such materials). Enrichment clusters can be designed in this manner as well, with a teacher selecting a math topic that is his or her specialty and area of interest. Students with high interest can work together over the course of several weeks exploring this topic.

Extracurricular Options

Programs that are extracurricular but often connected to, or at least taking place at, the school include math competitions such as Math Olympiad and the Continental Math League for elementary and middle school students, Math Counts for middle school students, and International Math Olympiad for high schoolers (see the resources section for further information). Often teachers coach students during designated enrichment blocks or after school to prepare for these competitions. The problems are quite challenging, and for students who enjoy competition, these opportunities can be motivational and enriching.

Afterschool math clubs and Saturday programs are other sources of motivation and enrichment for students. Again, using appropriate advanced curriculum resources similar to the ones mentioned for pull-out programs above will benefit students.

Out-of-School Programs

In addition, there are high-level advanced summer, weekend, and distance learning programs that offer accelerated, fast-paced courses and programs to highly talented math students in elementary through high school. Many universities conduct talent searches, such as Carnegie Mellon University, the University of Iowa, Duke University, Northwestern University, Stanford University, and Johns Hopkins University (see the resources section for further information). Qualifying students are then offered opportunities to take advanced math programs. Many of these programs use a Diagnostic Testing→Prescriptive Instruction Model, which involves individual testing, placement into an accelerated math course with a mentor, and testing to advance to the next level or course. There are generally costs involved, but for some programs, scholarships are available. Because the focus of these programs is acceleration, it is good advice to consult with school administrators and teachers to arrange for course credit and/or advancement to the next grade level curriculum or course upon satisfactory completion of an online course or program.

As previously discussed, working with a mentor is another way to enrich talented students. This can range from having rather informal regular meetings, to exploring an advanced topic of interest, to having more formal meetings, such as Math Circles. Math Circles began in Russia and were introduced in this country about 12 years ago. They are becoming increasingly popular, and there is a National Association of Math Circles. The purpose of Math Circles is to bring mathematicians, mathematical scientists, and high school students (and sometimes their teachers) together in an informal setting to work on interesting problems in mathematics. The goal of Math Circles is to provide a setting that encourages high school students to become passionate about mathematics. There are many mathematics professors who find joy in nurturing a mathematical mind and working with someone who is as passionate about mathematics as they are. Thus, opportunities to create mentorships should be pursued.

Finally, students can engage in programs of more intense study during the summer. Mentor Connection at the University of Connecticut and PROMYS at Boston University are some examples of programs open to talented high school students where students work intensely with mentors at universities on research projects and interesting problems.

In order to help talented students develop their mathematical gifts, there are many aspects to consider. The following tips provide a summary of the salient points previously mentioned and give teachers some concrete starting points to help identify talented students, find challenging and motivating curriculum for them, and provide a program that will foster an optimal learning environment.

Identification

Teachers should view themselves as math talent scouts, always on the lookout for new students.
- Look for behavioral characteristics in students that show a mathematical way of looking at the world (e.g., a high level of curiosity about numbers and patterns, unusual solutions to problems, enjoyment of challenging math problems and puzzles).
- Spot developing mathematical talent in students early, and continue as students move across grade levels.

- Use a variety of measures to identify students (e.g., tests, interviews, performance tasks, rating scales).
- Identify talent in students from all backgrounds, races, and ethnicities, especially in disadvantaged urban and rural areas.

Curriculum for Talented Students

Students deserve and need to learn something new in math class every day.

- Curriculum should be research-based, showing significant achievement gains for talented students over a comparison peer group.
- Curriculum should be above grade level and appropriate to the student's ability level.
- Curriculum should investigate challenging math problems.
- Curriculum should engage students to think deeply about mathematics.
- Curriculum should be motivational and should stimulate interest and a love of mathematics.
- Curriculum should encourage rich mathematical discussions among a peer group of talented students.
- Curriculum should provide opportunities for students to write about mathematical understanding and creative approaches to solving problems, akin to the practices of mathematicians.

Programming for Talented Students

Talented math students need opportunities to work and learn with students of similar abilities and interests.

- Group talented students together for math instruction.
- Search for math professors and other math professionals eager to work with talented students and set up mentoring opportunities.

- Start an Enrichment Math Club.
- Start a Math Circle.
- Join a local, national, or international math competition.
- Research summer programs for your talented students.
- Look for scholarships for special programs for your talented students.
- Research specialized schools for your talented students.
- Research opportunities for taking college courses during high school for your talented students.

Community

Last, but certainly not least, we must remember the words of Winston Churchill: "Attitude is a little thing that makes a big difference."

- Promote a positive attitude towards mathematics and mathematically talented people.
- Encourage your community, including local and state governments, to advertise the positive aspects of learning mathematics and the enjoyment that comes from engaging with mathematical problem solving.

Resources

Listed in this section are select resources for teachers and parents. For more information on STEM resources, including research references, see the "STEM: Meeting a Critical Demand for Excellence" page at the National Association for Gifted Children's website at http://www.nagc.org/index.aspx?id=1484.

Books, Book Chapters, and Research Resources

Assouline, S., & Lupkowski-Shoplik, A. (2011). *Developing math talent: A comprehensive guide to math education for gifted students in elementary and middle school* (2nd ed.). Waco, TX: Prufrock Press.

This book offers a comprehensive guide to educating gifted and talented students for success in math. Concrete suggestions for identifying talented students, tools for instructional planning, and programming options are outlined.

Colangelo, N., Assouline, S. G., & Gross, M. U. (2004). *A nation deceived: How schools hold back America's brightest students* (Vol. 1). Iowa City: University of Iowa, The Connie

Belin & Jacqueline N. Blank International Center for Gifted Education and Talent Development.

Colangelo, N., Assouline, S. G., & Gross, M. U. (Eds.). (2004). *A nation deceived: How schools hold back America's brightest students* (Vol. 2). Iowa City: University of Iowa, The Connie Belin & Jacqueline N. Blank International Center for Gifted Education and Talent Development.

This two-volume series comprises the Templeton National Report on the issues associated with acceleration in its many forms and the research that has been conducted on acceleration.

Gavin, M. K., & Adelson, J. L. (2007). Mathematics, elementary. In J. A. Plucker & C. M. Callahan (Eds.), *Critical issues and practices in gifted education: What the research says* (pp. 367–394). Washington, DC: National Association for Gifted Children.

Saul, M., Assouline, S., & Sheffield, L. J. (Eds.). (2010). *The peak in the middle: Developing mathematically gifted students in the middle grades.* Reston, VA: National Council of Teachers of Mathematics.

This book provides the rationale for offering advanced mathematics in the middle grades as well as the practical information that school leaders need for identifying and serving talented students.

Sriraman, B., & Steinthorsdottir, O. B. (2007). Mathematics, secondary. In J. A. Plucker & C. M. Callahan (Eds.), *Critical issues and practices in gifted education: What the research says* (pp. 367–394). Washington, DC: National Association for Gifted Children.

These two chapters are part of 50 summaries of important topics included in this reference book on giftedness and gifted education. The chapters provide relevant research on gifted mathematics education at the elementary and secondary levels and how the research applies to educating gifted students.

National Council of Teachers of Mathematics. (2000). *Principles and standards for school mathematics.* Reston, VA: Author.

Originally published in 1989, this revised book is the seminal work in mathematics education for curriculum and instruction for students in grades K–12 throughout the United States. Five content strands and five process standards are delineated across grade level bands with explanations and illustrated examples.

Sheffield, L. J. (1994). *The development of gifted and talented mathematics students and the National Council of Teachers of Mathematics Standards.* Storrs: University of Connecticut, The National Research Center for the Gifted and Talented.

This monograph presents the need for and ways to develop mathematically talented students in elementary, middle, and high schools. The status of mathematical talent in the United States and international comparisons are discussed. Identification of mathematical giftedness, programming options, curriculum, teaching, and assessment are all addressed with connections to the National Council of Teachers of Mathematics standards.

Sheffield, L. J. (Ed.). (1999). *Developing mathematically promising students.* Reston, VA: National Council of Teachers of Mathematics.

Written by leading experts in mathematics education and gifted education, this book is a compilation of chapters on various aspects of gifted mathematics education, including identification, gender issues, curriculum, and programming.

Waxman, B., Robinson, N. M., & Mukhopadhyay, S. (1996). *Teachers nurturing math-talented young children.* Storrs: University of Connecticut, The National Research Center for the Gifted and Talented.

This monograph is an outgrowth of a 2-year study of mathematically advanced children during preschool and kindergarten. The
monograph discusses ways of organizing classes and schools to
support the development of these children. It describes a philosophy of teaching mathematics and open-ended teaching methods
that make it possible. In addition, sample open-ended activities
and literature connections are presented.

Curriculum Resources

Gavin, M. K., Chapin, S. H., Dailey, J., & Sheffield, L. J. (2006–
   2010). *Project M³: Mentoring mathematical minds.* Dubuque, IA:
   Kendall Hunt.

This is an NAGC award-winning series of 12 research-based
units of accelerated and enriched mathematical content for talented math students at the elementary level, funded by a U.S.
Department of Education Javits Grant:

Level 3 Units:
- *Unraveling the Mystery of the MoLi Stone: Place Value and
  Numeration*
- *Awesome Algebra: Looking for Patterns and Generalizations*
- *What's the ME in Measurement All About?*
- *Digging for Data: The Search Within Research*

Level 4 Units:
- *Factors, Multiples, and Leftovers: Linking Multiplication and
  Division*
- *At the Mall With Algebra: Working With Variables and
  Equations*
- *Getting Into Shapes*
- *Analyze This! Representing and Interpreting Data*

Level 5 Units:
- *Treasures From the Attic: Exploring Fractions*
- *Record Makers and Breakers: Using Algebra to Analyze Change*

- *Funkytown Fun House: Focusing on Proportional Reasoning and Similarity*
- *What Are Your Chances?*

Gavin, M. K., Casa, T. M., Chapin, S. H., & Sheffield, L. J. (2010–2012). *Project M²: Mentoring Young Mathematicians.* Dubuque, IA: Kendall Hunt.

This is an NAGC award-winning series of six units of research-based advanced curriculum in geometry and measurement for students in grades K–2, funded by a National Science Foundation grant:

Level 2 Units:
- *Designing a Shape Gallery: Geometry With the Meerkats*
- *Using Everyday Measures: Measuring With the Meerkats*

Level 1 Units:
- *Exploring Shape Games: Geometry With Imi and Zani*
- *Creating the School Measurement Fair: Measuring With Imi and Zani*

Level Kindergarten Units:
- *Exploring Shapes in Space: Geometry With the Frogonauts*
- *Sizing Up the Lily Pad Space Station: Measuring With the Frogonauts*

Supplemental Curriculum Resources

Burger, E. B., & Starbird, M. (2005) *The heart of mathematics: An invitation to effective thinking.* Emeryville, CA: Key College.

This resource is particularly useful for small group/individual investigations with talented middle school students. It includes a variety of interesting math topics outside of the regular curriculum, such as topology, chaos and fractals, and the study of infinity.

Findell, C. R., Gavin, M. K., Greenes, C. E., & Sheffield, L. J. (2000). *Awesome math problems for creative thinking*. Chicago, IL: Creative Publications.

This resource is a series of six books of interesting nonroutine problems in number, algebraic thinking, geometry, measurement, data analysis, and probability, specifically designed for talented math students in grades 3–8.

Sheffield, L. J. (2003) *Extending the challenge in mathematics: Developing mathematical promise in K–8 students*. Thousand Oaks, CA: Corwin Press.

The multilevel investigations in this book are designed to challenge students in the areas of number, algebra, geometry and measurement, data analysis, and probability. Strategies for assessment are included.

National Programs, Institutes, and Universities That Promote Development of Mathematical Talent

Boston University: PROMYS Program

http://www.promys.org

PROMYS is a challenging 6-week summer program designed to encourage ambitious high school students to explore the creative world of mathematics with mentors including research mathematicians.

Carnegie Mellon University: Carnegie Mellon Institute for Talented Elementary and Secondary Students (C-Mites)

http://www.cmu.edu/cmites

This institute provides challenging weekend workshops and summer programs for students in grades K–9.

Drexel University: Math Forum

http://mathforum.org

Math Forum is an excellent online resource with a wealth of problems and puzzles, online mentoring, research, team problem solving, collaborations, and professional development.

Duke University: Talent Identification Program (Duke TIP)

http://www.tip.duke.edu

The Duke TIP conducts talent searches and offers summer courses, scholar weekends, independent study courses, and online courses including courses in mathematics.

Expanding Your Horizons in Science and Mathematics

http://www.expandingyourhorizons.org

This program hosts, organizes, and offers conferences to nurture girls' interest in science and math courses to encourage them to consider careers in science, technology, engineering, and math.

Johns Hopkins University: The Center for Talented Youth

http://cty.jhu.edu

The Center for Talented Youth focuses on the needs of students with exceptionally high academic abilities, including mathematically gifted youth. The Center conducts the nation's oldest university-based talent search for highly able youth, offers 3-week residential and day programs for students in grades 2–12 at various sites across the country, provides academically challenging online courses for students in grades K–12, and offers family academic programs and counseling services.

Northwestern University: The Center for Talent Development

http://www.ctd.northwestern.edu

The Center for Talent Development conducts talent searches and has a range of programs for gifted students, including summer programs, Saturday enrichment programs, and online accelerated courses such as AP and honors mathematics courses.

Stanford University: The Education Program for Gifted Youth (EPGY)

http://epgy.stanford.edu

This program is dedicated to developing and offering multimedia computer-based distance-learning courses. EPGY provides high-ability students of all ages with an individualized educational experience, optimized in both pace and content. The program has recently inaugurated an online high school, a 3-year diploma-granting school.

University of Connecticut: Neag Center for Gifted Education and Talent Development

http://www.gifted.uconn.edu/projectm3

Information on Project M^3 curriculum units (Grades 3–5) is available at this website, as well as tips, resources, and links to problem-solving sites for students, parents, and teachers.

http://projectm2.uconn.edu

Information on Project M^2 curriculum units (Grades K–2) is available at this website, as well as tips, resources, and links to problem-solving sites for students, parents, and teachers.

http://www.gifted.uconn.edu/mentor

Information on Mentor Connection, an annual 3-week residential summer program at the University of Connecticut for academically talented secondary students to develop creative productivity, is available at this website. Mentors include research mathematicians and scientists.

University of Iowa: The Belin-Blank Center

http://www.education.uiowa.edu/belinblank

The Belin-Blank Center conducts a talent search and offers summer programs with math courses for talented students and an online AP academy including AP mathematics courses.

Mathematics Competitions

The following is a list of websites that offer information about mathematics competitions for talented students in elementary, middle, and high schools.

American Mathematics Competitions (AMC)

http://amc.maa.org

Continental Math League

http://www.continentalmathematicsleague.com

International Mathematical Olympiad (IMO)

http://imo.math.ca

MATHCOUNTS (Middle School Competition)

http://mathcounts.org

Mandelbrot Competition

http://www.mandelbrot.org

Mathematical Olympiads for Elementary and Middle Schools (MOEMS)

http://www.moems.org

Math League
http://www.themathleague.com

USA Mathematical Talent Search (USAMTS)
http://www.usamts.org

National Organizations

The following is a list of national organizations related to mathematics, mathematics education, and gifted education.

American Mathematical Society
http://www.ams.org

The Art of Problem Solving Foundation
http://www.artofproblemsolving.org

Association for Women in Mathematics (AWM)
http://sites.google.com/site/awmmath

Davidson Fellows Scholarships
http://www.davidsongifted.org/fellows

National Association for Gifted Children
http://www.nagc.org

National Association of Math Circles
http://www.mathcircles.org

National Consortium for Specialized Secondary Schools of Mathematics, Science & Technology
http://www.ncsssmst.org

National Council of Supervisors of Mathematics
http://www.mathedleadership.org

National Council of Teachers of Mathematics
http://www.nctm.org

Additional Websites

The following websites have extensive listings of organizations, competitions, games, problem-solving websites, printed materials, summer and online programs, and other links to develop mathematical talent for creative and promising mathematics students.

Davidson Institute
http://davidsongifted.org
To access mathematics resources on this site, type "mathematics" into the search field.

Mathematics Education at Northern Kentucky University
http://www.nku.edu/~mathed/gifted.html

Assouline, S., Colangelo, N., Lupkowski-Shoplik, A., Lipscomb, J., & Forstadt, L. (2003). *Iowa Acceleration Scale: Manual, form, and summary and planning sheet.* Scottsdale, AZ: Great Potential Press.

Carroll, S. R. (2010). *M² student mathematics performance: 1st grade summation evaluation (PY2).* Torrington, CT: Words & Numbers Research.

Colangelo, N., Assouline, S. G., & Gross, M. U. (2004). *A nation deceived: How schools hold back America's brightest students* (Vol. 2). Iowa City: University of Iowa, The Connie Belin & Jacqueline N. Blank International Center for Gifted Education and Talent Development.

Davidson, J. E., & Sternberg, R. J. (1984). The role of insight in intellectual giftedness. *Gifted Child Quarterly, 28,* 58–64.

Dixon, F. A., Gallagher, S. A., & Olszewski-Kubilius, P. A. (2009). A visionary statement for the education of gifted students in secondary schools. In F. A. Dixon (Ed.), *Programs and services for gifted secondary students: A guide to recommend practices* (pp. 173–184). Waco, TX: Prufrock Press.

Feldhusen, J. F., Hoover, S. M., & Sayler, M. F. (1989). *Identification of gifted students at the secondary level.* Monroe, NY: Trillium Press.

Gavin, M. K. (2005, Fall/Winter). Are we missing anyone? Identifying mathematically promising students. *Gifted Education Communicator,* 24–29.

Gavin, M. K. (2010). Mathematics characteristics. In J. S. Renzulli, L. H. Smith, A. J. White, C. M. Callahan, R. K. Hartman, K. L. Westberg, M. K. Gavin, S. M. Reis, D. Siegle, & R. E. Sytsma Reed. *Scales for Rating the Behavioral Characteristics of Superior Students* (3rd ed.). Mansfield Center, CT: Creative Learning Press.

Gavin, M. K., & Adelson, J. L. (2008). Mathematics, elementary. In J. A. Plucker & C. M. Callahan (Eds.), *Critical issues and practices in gifted education: What the research says* (pp. 367–394). Washington, DC: National Association for Gifted Children.

Gavin, M. K., Casa, T., Adelson, J., Carroll, S. R., & Sheffield, L. J. (2009). The impact of advanced curriculum on the achievement of mathematically promising elementary students. *Gifted Child Quarterly, 53*(3), 188–202.

Gavin, M. K., Casa, T. M., Adelson, J. L., Carroll, S. R., Sheffield, L. J., & Spinelli, A. M. (2007). Project M^3: Mentoring mathematical minds: A research-based curriculum for talented elementary students. *Journal of Advanced Academics, 18*(4), 566–585.

Gavin, M. K., Casa, T. M., Chapin, S., & Sheffield, L. J. (2011). *Project M²: Exploring shape games: Geometry with Imi and Zani.* Dubuque, IA: Kendall Hunt.

Gavin, M. K., Chapin, S. H., Sheffield, L. J., & Dailey, J. (2008). *Project M^3: What are your chances?* Dubuque, IA: Kendall/Hunt.

Gavin, M. K., & Sheffield, L. J. (2010). Using curriculum to develop mathematical promise in the middle grades. In M. Saul, S. Assouline, & L. J. Sheffield (Eds.), *The peak in the middle: Developing mathematically gifted students in the middle grades* (pp. 51–76). Reston, VA: National Council of Teachers of Mathematics.

Gavin, M. K., Sheffield, L. J., & Chapin, S. H. (2010). *Math innovations, level 3: Solve it: Focusing on equations, inequalities, and exponents.* Dubuque, IA: Kendall/Hunt.

Gilliam, J. E., Carpenter, B. O., & Christensen, J. R. (1996). *Gifted and talented evaluation scales.* Austin, TX: PRO-ED.

Kerr, B. A. (1997). Developing talent in girls and young women. In N. Colangelo & G. A. Davis (Eds.), *Handbook of gifted education* (2nd ed.; pp. 483–497). Boston, MA: Allyn & Bacon.

Krutetskii, V. A. (1976). *The psychology of mathematical abilities in schoolchildren* (J. Teller, Trans.). Chicago, IL: University of Chicago Press. (Original work published in 1968)

Kuenzi, J. J. (2008). *Science, technology, engineering, and mathematics (STEM) education: Background, federal policy, and legislative action.* Washington, DC: Congressional Research Service.

McCarney, S. B., & Anderson, P. D. (1998). *The gifted evaluation scale* (2nd ed.). Columbia, MO: Hawthorne Educational Services.

Montana Council of Teachers of Mathematics. (2006). *SIMMS integrated mathematics, level 3.* Dubuque, IA: Kendall/Hunt.

National Assessment of Educational Progress. (2008). *The nation's report card: Mathematics 2007.* Retrieved from http://nationsreportcard.gov/math_2009

National Center for Education Statistics. (2008). *Highlights from TIMMS 2007.* Retrieved from http://nces.ed.gov/pubs2009/2009001.pdf

National Center for Education Statistics. (2010). *Digest of education statistics, 2009* (NCES 2010-013). Retrieved from http://nces.ed.gov/programs/digest/d09/tables/dt09_271.asp

National Research Council. (2002). *Learning and understanding: Improving advanced study of mathematics and science in US high schools.* Washington, DC: National Academy Press.

National Science Board. (2010). *Preparing the next generation of STEM innovators: Identifying and developing our nation's human capital* (NSB-10-33). Arlington, VA: National Science Foundation.

Reis, S. M., Burns, D. E., & Renzulli, J. S. (1992). *Curriculum compacting: The complete guide to modifying the curriculum for high ability students.* Mansfield Center, CT: Creative Learning Press.

Renzulli, J. S., Smith, L. H., White, A. J., Callahan, C. M., Hartman, R. K., Westberg, K. L., Gavin, M. K., Reis, S. M., Siegle, D., & Sytsma Reed, R. E. *Scales for rating the behavioral characteristics of superior students* (3rd ed.). (2004). Mansfield Center, CT: Creative Learning Press.

Renzulli, J. S., Siegle, D., Reis, S. M., Gavin, M. K., & Sytsma Reed, R. E. (2009). An investigation of the reliability and factor structure of four new scales for rating the behavioral characteristics of superior students. *Journal of Advanced Academics, 21*(1), 84–108.

Renzulli, J. S., Smith, L. H., White, A. J., Callahan, C. M., & Hartman, R. K. (1976). *Scales for rating the behavioral characteristics of superior students.* Mansfield Center, CT: Creative Learning Press.

Robinson, N. M., & Weimer, L. J. (1991). Selection of candidates for early admission to kindergarten and first grade. In W. T. Southern & E. D. Jones (Eds.), *The academic acceleration of gifted children* (pp. 29–73). New York, NY: Teachers College Press.

Rogers, K. B. (1991). *The relationship of grouping practices to the education of the gifted and talented learner* (Research Monograph No. 9102). Storrs: University of Connecticut, The National Research Center on the Gifted and Talented.

Rogers, K. B. (1992). A best-evidence synthesis of the research on acceleration options for gifted learners. In N. Colangelo, S. G. Assouline, & D. L. Ambroson (Eds.), *Talent development: Proceedings from the 1991 Henry B. and Jocelyn Wallace National Research Symposium on Talent Development* (pp. 406–409). Unionville, NY: Trillium.

Sheffield, L. J., Bennett, J., Berriozabal, M., DeArmond, M., & Wertheimer, R. (1999). Report of the task force on the mathematically promising. In L. J. Sheffield (Ed.), *Developing mathematically promising students* (pp. 309–316). Reston, VA: National Council of Teachers of Mathematics.

Sriraman, B., & Steinthorsdottir, O. B. (2008). Mathematics, secondary. In J. A. Plucker & C. M. Callahan (Eds.), *Critical issues and practices in gifted education: What the research says* (pp. 395–407). Waco, TX: Prufrock Press.

Subotnik, R., Edmiston, A., & Rayhack, K. (2007). Developing national policies in STEM talent development: Obstacles and opportunities. In P. Csermely, K. Korlevic, & K. Sulyok (Eds.), *Science education: Models and networking of student research training under 21* (pp. 28–38). Netherlands: IOS Press.

Tieso, C. L. (2002). *The effects of grouping and curricular practices on intermediate students' math achievement* (Research Monograph No. 02154). Storrs: University of Connecticut, The National Research Center on the Gifted and Talented.

Tomlinson, C. A. (1995). Deciding to differentiate instruction in middle school: One school's journey. *Gifted Child Quarterly, 39*, 77–87.

VanTassel-Baska, J. (2005). *Acceleration strategies for teaching gifted learners*. Waco, TX: Prufrock Press.

M. Katherine Gavin, Ph.D., is an Associate Professor at the University of Connecticut, where she serves as the math specialist at the Neag Center for Gifted Education and Talent Development. She is the principal investigator and senior author of two national research projects that involve the development of advanced mathematics units for mathematically talented students in grades K–5. Project M^3 units, developed under a Jacob K. Javits U.S. Department of Education research grant, have won the NAGC Curriculum Division Award for 6 consecutive years. Published by Kendall Hunt, they are being used in all 50 states and in nations including Singapore, Canada, and the Netherlands. Dr. Gavin and her colleagues also received the 2009 Research Paper of the Year award from *Gifted Child Quarterly*, the leading United States research journal in gifted education, for an article that reported the research results of Project M^3. Project M^2, Mentoring Young Mathematicians, is a National Science Foundation project currently underway whose purpose is to develop and research advanced curriculum for primary students. This project recently received the 2010 NAGC Curriculum Division Award. Dr. Gavin is also a coauthor and project director of a new middle school textbook series, *Math Innovations*, published by Kendall Hunt. She received the Early Leader Award from NAGC in 2006.

A former mathematics teacher, department chair, and district coordinator, Dr. Gavin has written numerous articles and book chapters on gifted mathematics education, is a member of the writing team for the NCTM *Navigations* series, and has coauthored a series of creative problem-solving books. In addition, as a consultant, she provides professional development for teachers and administrators in school districts across the country and presents annually at national and international conferences.

Printed in the United States
by Baker & Taylor Publisher Services